NATIONAL GEOGRAPHIC

A Dog's Life

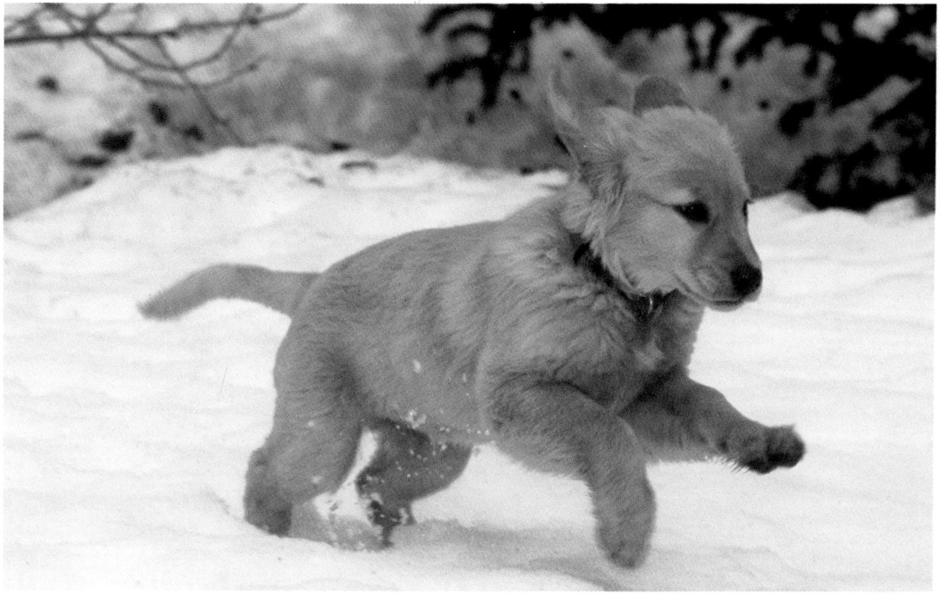

Rose Lorenzo

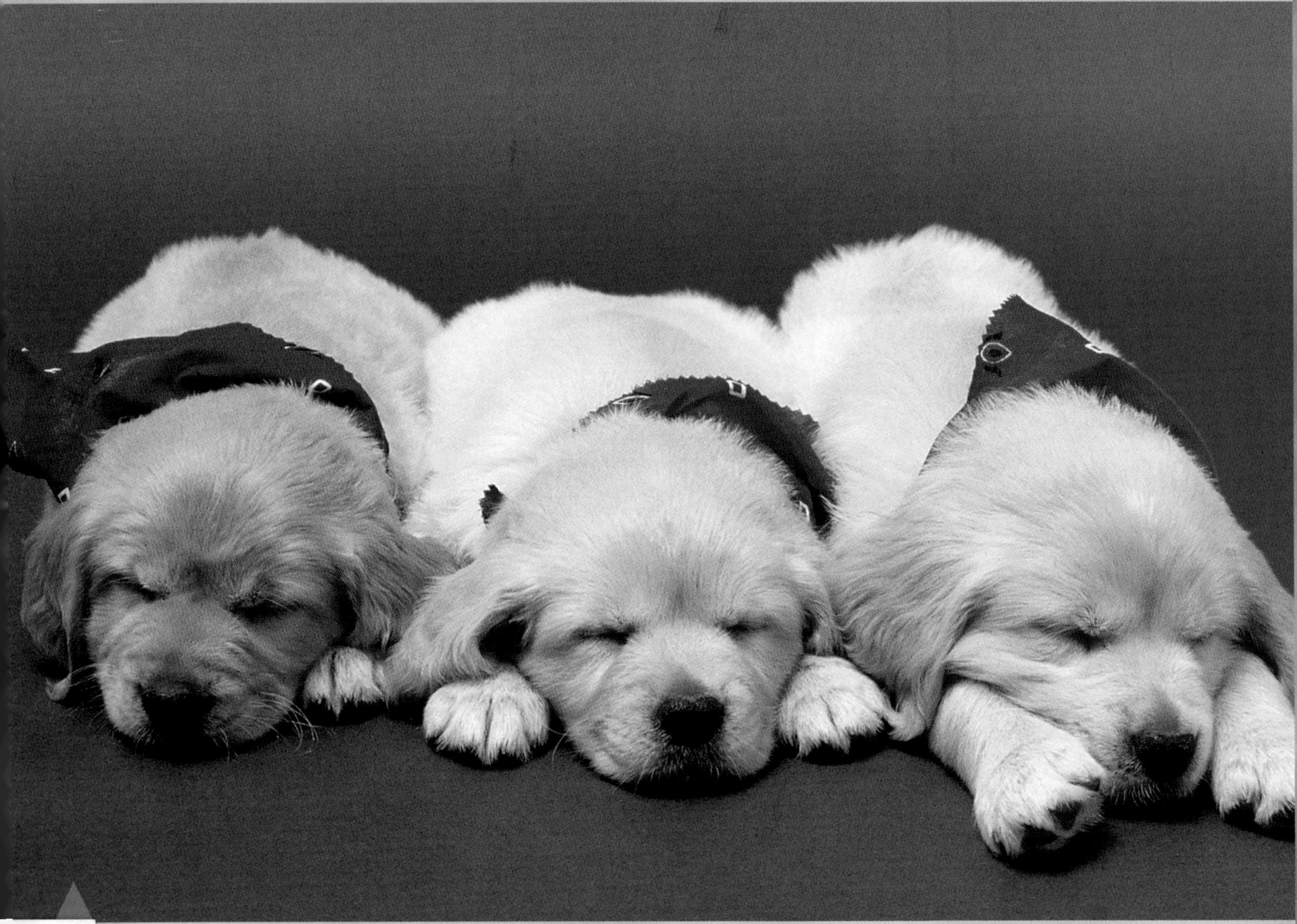

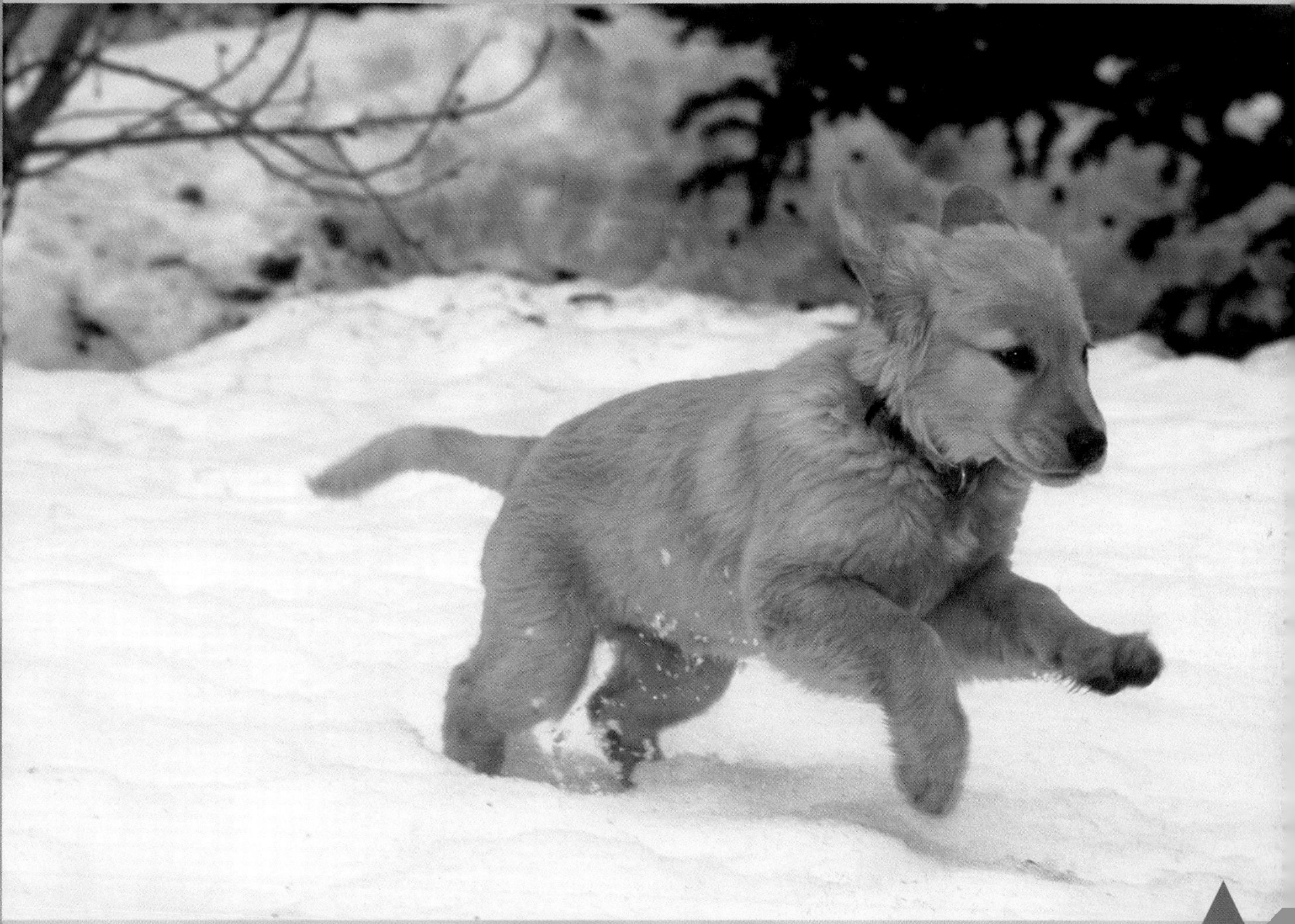

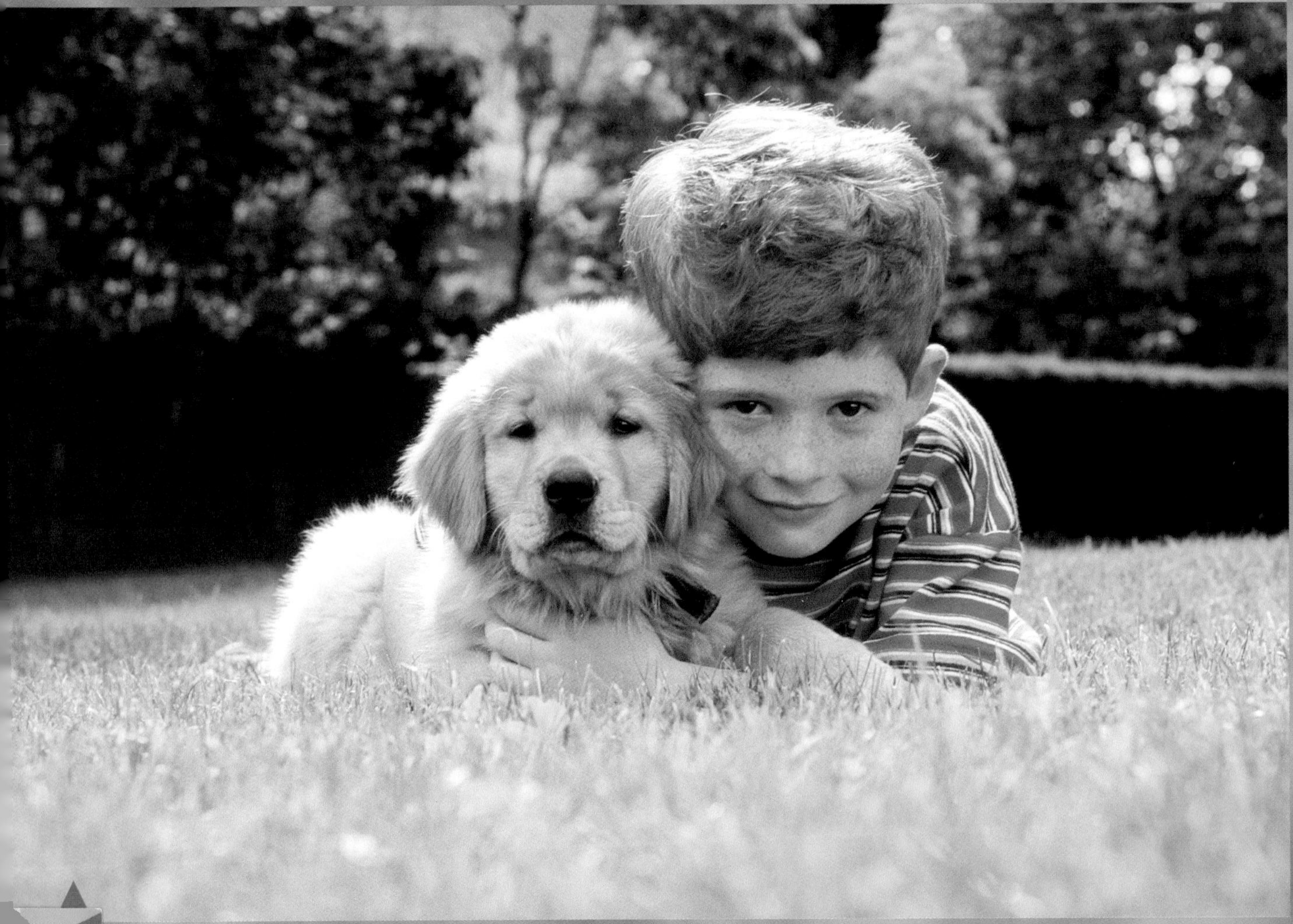

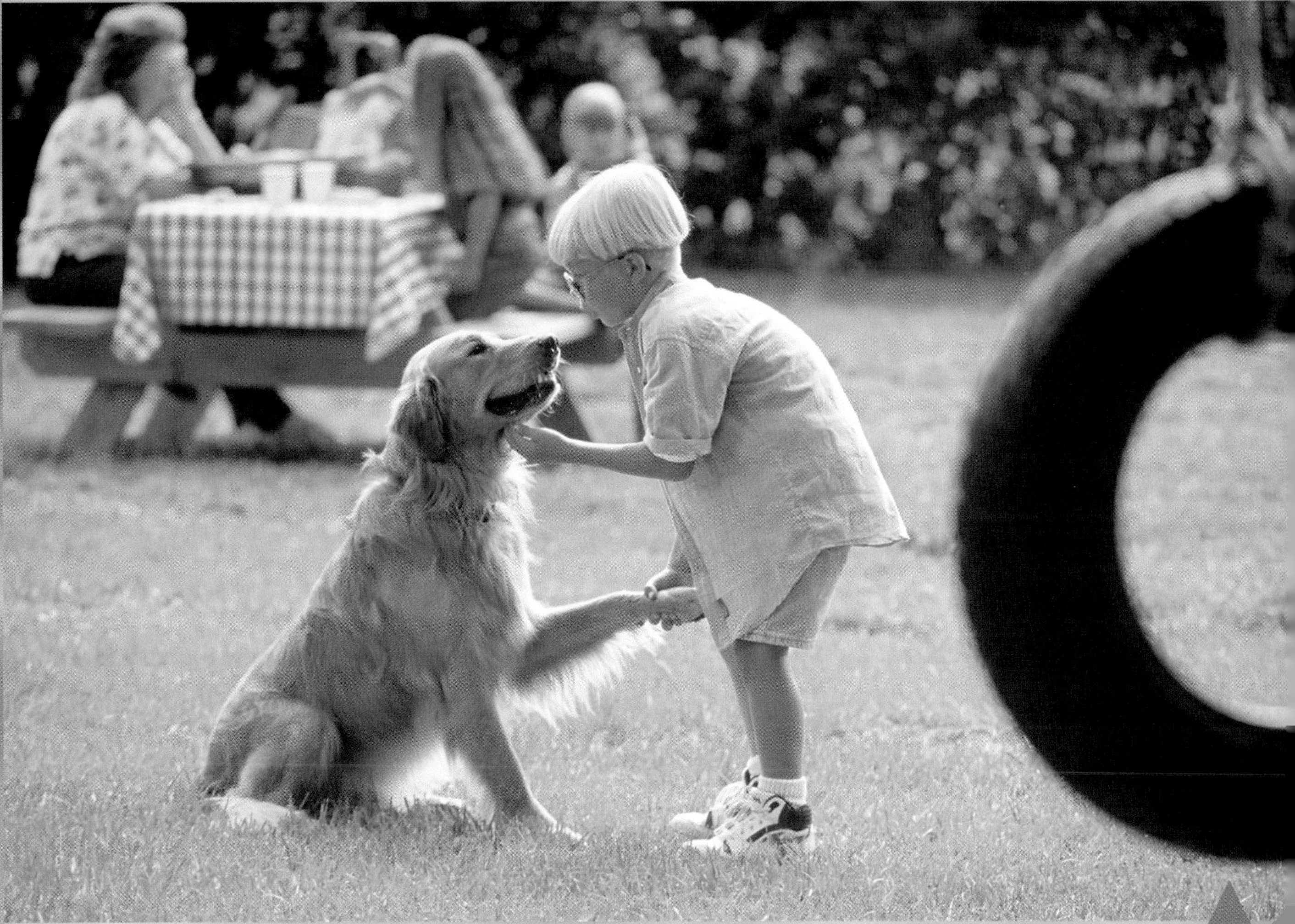

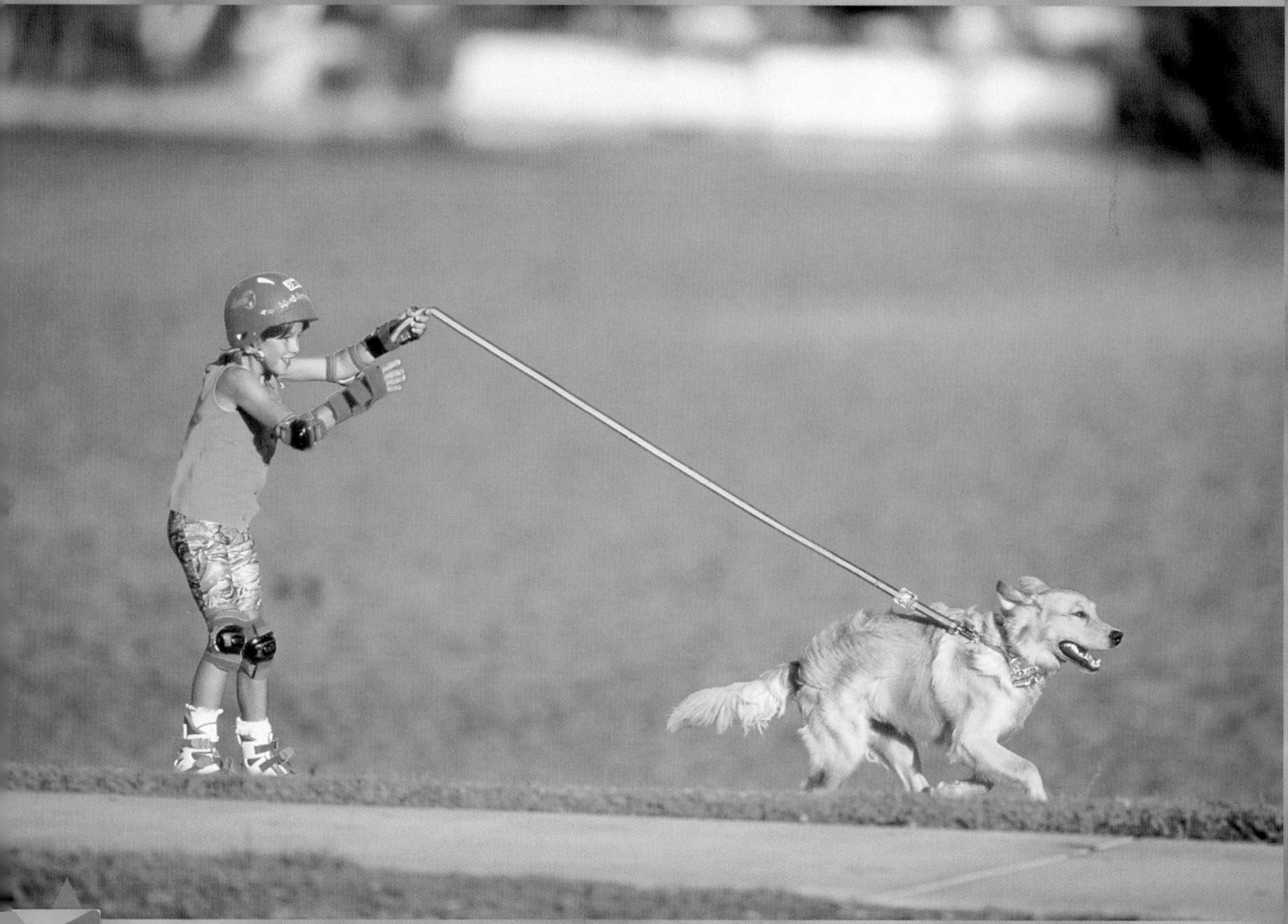

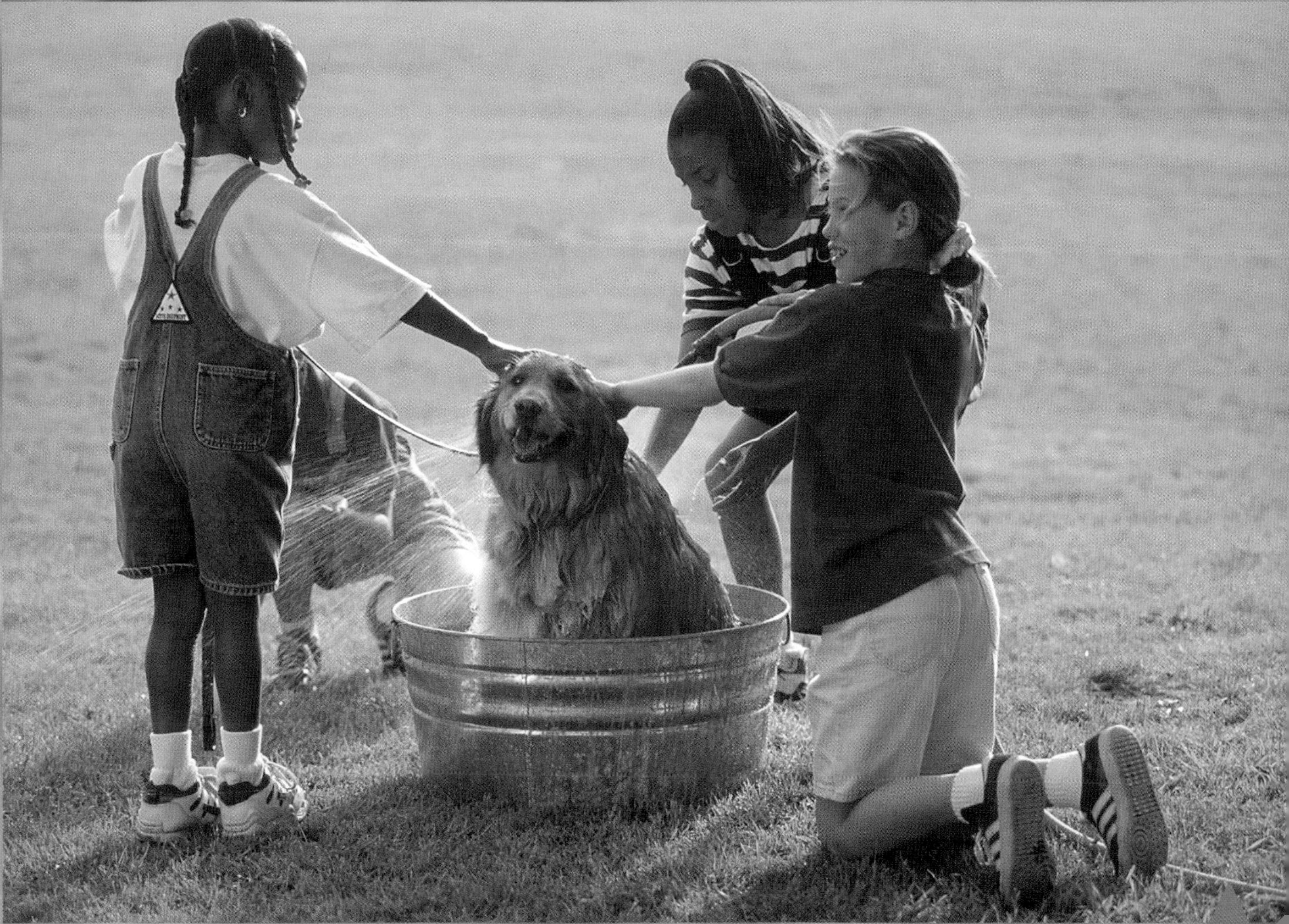

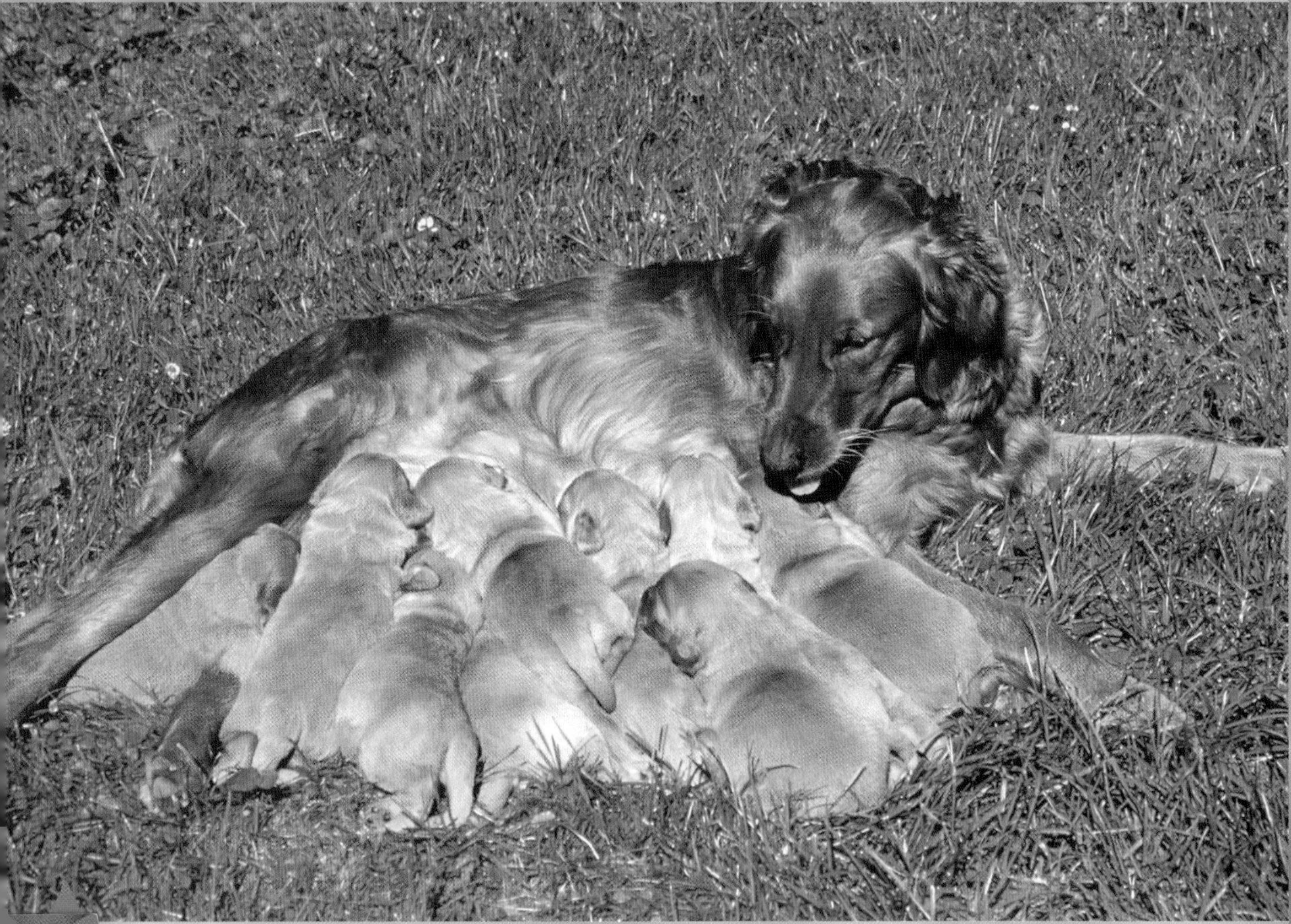